How Do We Feel and Touch?

Carol Ballard

WAYLAND

How Our Bodies Work

How Do Our Eyes See?

How Do Our Ears Hear?

How Do We Taste and Smell?

How Do We Feel and Touch?

How Do We Think?

How Do We Move?

Editor: Ruth Raudsepp
Illustrators: Kevin Jones Associates and Michael Courtney
Designer: Phil Jackson

First published in 1997 by Wayland Publishers Ltd, 61 Western Road,
Hove, East Sussex, BN3 1JD, England.
© Copyright 1997 Wayland Publishers Ltd

Find Wayland on the internet at http://www.wayland.co.uk

British Library Cataloguing in Publication Data
Ballard, Carol
How Do We Feel and Touch? – (How Our Bodies Work)
1. Touch – Juvenile literature
I. Title II. Jones, K. III Courtney, M.
612.8'8

ISBN 0 7502 2069 4

Picture acknowledgements
The author and publishers thank the following for use of their photographs:
Action-Plus 25 (top); Allsport 23 (top); Bubbles *title page*, 18, 23 (bottom), 25;
Zul/Chapel Studios 5 (top), 12, 14, 16, 19, 21; Bruce Coleman 28; Greg Evans 4, 20;
Chris Fairclough 6, 27; Impact 5 (bottom); NHPA 10; Oxford Scientific Films 29;
Science Photo Library 26.

Typeset by Phil Jackson
Printed in Italy by G Canale & C. S. p. A.

Contents

Touching

Our sense of touch is important. We use it to collect information about the world around us. Imagine you are given something you have never seen before. You could find out about it just by touching it. Is it hard like metal or rough like the bark of a tree? Is it sharp and prickly like a hedgehog or soft like a kitten's fur?

▲ Our skin feels cold in winter. This boy is blowing into his hands to warm them.

◀ What do you think the tree bark feels like under this girl's hands?

Our sense of touch helps to keep us safe. For example, if you put your hand on something very hot, you react instantly by pulling your hand away before it gets burned.

Blind people rely on their sense of touch. Many things that they use, such as knobs on cookers, have raised bumps for them to feel rather than see.

This book tells you about your sense of touch and how it works.

▲ These girls are wearing dresses made of velvet. Velvet feels very soft and smooth.

5

Does dry sand feel the same as ▶ wet sand?

Inside the skin

Skin forms a protective covering. It stops harmful things getting into the body. It helps control body temperature and the amount of water lost through sweating. **Receptor** cells in the skin allow us to feel the objects we touch.

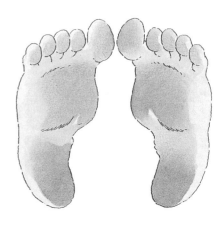

▲
The outer layer of skin is much thicker on our feet than anywhere else on our bodies.

There are two main layers of skin. The outer layer is called the **epidermis**. It is made up of dead cells which get worn away by our every day activities, so it is constantly being replaced with new cells from the inner layer.

◄ Sunlight contains ultraviolet light which can be dangerous to our skin. To protect us our skin makes extra **pigment** – we develop a sun tan.

This is called the **dermis**. The inner layer contains **capillaries**, nerves and hairs. It also contains sweat glands and **ducts**, which carry sweat to the surface of the skin. Receptor cells are also in the dermis. Some are near to the surface while others are deeply buried. **Nerves** connect the receptor cells to the brain.

If you could look inside your skin ▼ with a microscope, it would look rather like this.

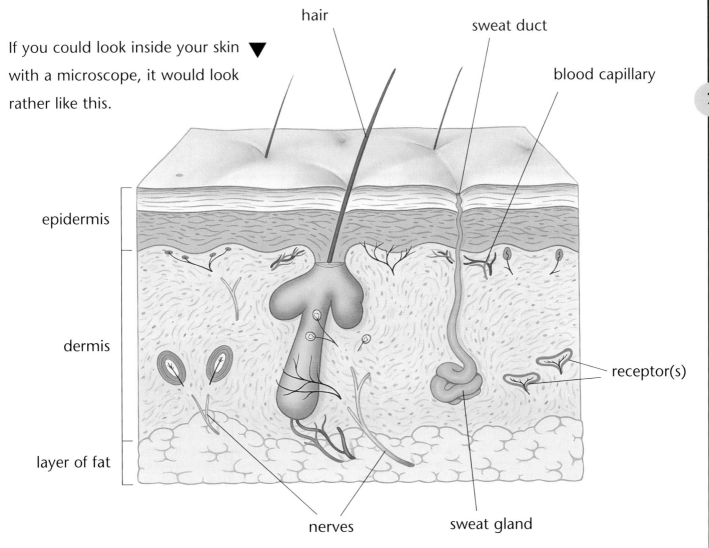

hair

sweat duct

blood capillary

epidermis

dermis

layer of fat

receptor(s)

nerves

sweat gland

How Do Receptors Work?

There are special types of receptors for touch, pressure, pain, hot and cold. Each receptor can only respond to its own special feeling. For example, if you put your hand into warm water, the hot receptors will respond but the cold receptors will not.

8

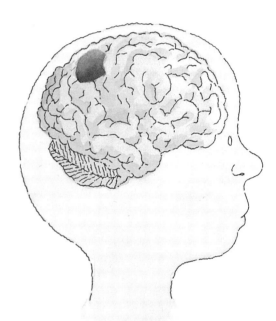

▲
Messages from receptor cells travel to the upper back part of the brain.

Some sensations involve more than one type of receptor. If you pick up something hot and sharp, both hot and pain receptors will respond.

When a receptor is **stimulated**, it responds by sending a message along nerves to the brain. The brain knows where the message came from, so it can tell exactly where the feeling is. It decides whether action is necessary and may send a message to the muscles telling them to move part of your body. This all happens in a fraction of a second so it seems as if you feel as soon as you touch.

Your nerves and brain ▶ react quickly to keep your body safe.

5. The brain sends a message to the muscles. You put the plate down instantly.

4. The brain interprets the message.

3. The message travels to the brain.

2. Hot receptors in the fingertips respond.

1. Pick up a hot plate

Light touch

If something touches you lightly, it makes contact with your skin but does not press hard. The shape of your skin does not change and the feeling usually only lasts for a short time.

▲

Even though the moth's wings are delicate, this boy can feel them brushing lightly over his hand.

There are different types of light touch receptor. The most common are free nerve endings. Others have a tiny disk attached to them or are surrounded by an egg-shaped protective case. Most receptors lie at the join between the two skin layers.

Some light touch receptors cluster around the ends of hairs and respond to movement of the hair. This means that you can feel something which touches your hair but not your skin.

Parts of the body have many light touch receptors so they are very **sensitive**. Other parts do not have as many, so they are less sensitive.

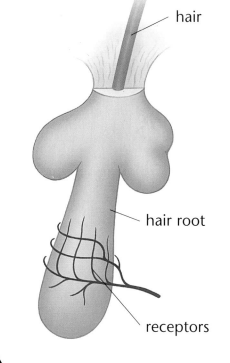

hair

hair root

receptors

There are different types of light-touch receptor. ▶

▼

▲

The receptors around a hair can detect very tiny hair movements.

Some receptors have free nerve endings.

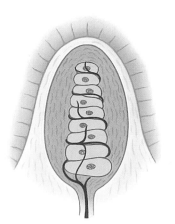

Some receptors have egg-shaped capsules.

Some receptors are like flat discs.

Make a Feely Box

How much can you find out just by feeling things? You can use a feely box to find out.

You will need a cardboard box with a lid. Mark and cut two holes in one side, big enough to put your hands through. Decorate the outside of the box if you want to.

▲ Objects that could go inside a feely box.

◄ These children are trying to find out what is inside the feely box.

Choose some small objects to put into the box. You could choose things with different textures. For example, a piece of bark, pebbles and spiky cones. You could choose things that have different shapes. For example, a smooth object such as a plastic ruler or pencil case. Or long bendy objects such as drinking straws or wool. Or you could make a collection of soft or round objects.

Put the objects in the box and put the lid back on. Ask friends to put their hands through the holes and pick up one object at a time. Keep a record of the objects they can and cannot identify. Do they find it easier to detect objects of different textures or different shapes?

Person \ Object	Bark	Seashell	Pebble	Eraser
Mark	✔	✗	✔	✗
Javed	✗	✔	✗	✔
Susan	✔	✔		
Ravinda	✔			
Mum	✔			

▲ Record your results on a table like this.

How Sensitive Are You?

Are some parts of your body are more sensitive to touch than others? Try this activity with a friend to find out. You will need a washable felt pen and a fine bristle from an old hairbrush.

Decide which parts of the body you want to test. The palm and back of your hand and the top and sole of your foot are ideal, but you could try other parts too.

◀ These children are trying to find out which is more sensitive; the palm of the hand or the back of the hand.

Mark a pattern of twenty small dots on the area to be tested. The person being tested must not look as you gently touch one of the dots with the bristle. Note when they feel the bristle and when they do not. Then do the same for other parts of the body.

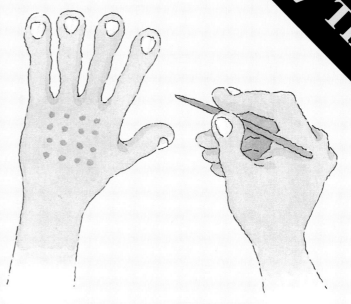

▲ If you draw a regular pattern of dots, it is much easier to keep track of which you have already tested.

15

Look at your results. Which part of the body was most sensitive and which was least sensitive?

When you have finished your test, draw ▶ a bar chart to show your results.

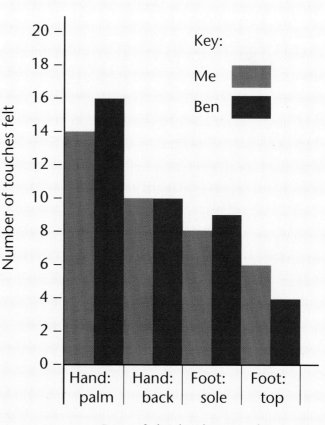

Pressure

If you press something hard, your skin will be squashed. This is different from just touching something lightly, and is detected by different receptors. The feeling of pressure usually lasts longer and is spread over a larger area than the feeling of light touch.

▲
We can often feel the sensation of pressure long after the object that caused it has been taken away.

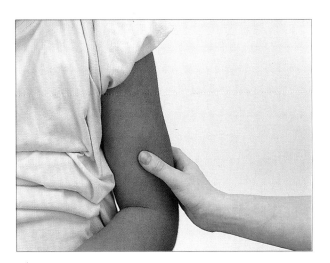

▲
The hand in this picture is resting lightly on the skin. The skin is not pushed out of shape. There is no pressure.

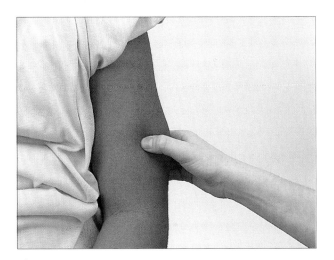

▲
The hand in this picture is pressing hard on the skin. Look at the way the skin is dented. There is pressure.

Most pressure receptors lie inside the dermis of the skin. Pressure receptors are usually larger than light touch receptors and are surrounded by a capsule. They measure tiny changes in pressure, rather than the actual pressure.

Pressure receptors also pick up **vibrations.** Some are sensitive to very fast vibrations and others to slow vibrations. Like light touch receptors, some pressure receptors cluster around hair shafts and pick up hair movements.

B receptors pick up fast vibrations

A capsule

C

B

capsule

nerve endings

nerve endings

Receptors **A** and **C** pick up slow vibrations

◄ These receptors all detect changes in pressure.

Itch and Tickle

Part of the body usually starts to itch when nerves in the skin are stimulated over and over again. Itches occur particularly around the eyes and nose.

Itches can also be caused by chemicals. When bitten by an insect, your body responds by releasing chemicals. These chemicals make your skin feel itchy. Some illnesses, such as chickenpox, also cause this sort of itch.

▲ Scratching a chemical itch will only make it worse.

◄ Treating an insect bite with the right ointment can take away itching.

18

When you scratch an itch, it usually feels better straight away. However, if it is a chemical itch, scratching could make it worse. The scratching irritates the skin, so more chemicals are released and the skin itches even more.

Many people are ticklish on their feet, the palms of their hands or the back of their neck.
A tickle is caused by the same sort of **stimulus** as an itch, although it is usually more gentle and moves across the surface of the skin.

Light, gentle movements ▶
can be very ticklish.

Hot and Cold

We cannot tell exactly how hot or cold something is, we can only compare the temperature to that of our skin.

We have two different types of temperature receptor. Hot receptors respond to things which are hotter than skin temperature. Cold receptors respond to things which are colder than skin temperature. The hot and cold receptors are free nerve endings. They lie at the top of the dermis, just below the epidermis.

▲ A thermometer can tell us the exact temperature. Our bodies can only compare the temperature with that of our skin.

◀ We cover and protect our bodies in winter but our faces are exposed all the time. Our face is less sensitive to cold than the rest of our body.

Hot and cold receptors are not spread evenly throughout the body. They are clustered together in hot spots, which respond to heat, and cold spots which respond to cold. The lips have hot spots and cold spots so they can detect both heat and cold. Our teeth are much more sensitive to cold than to heat.

This girl has her left hand in cold water and ▶ her right hand in hot water. If she then puts both hands into warm water, her brain will get confusing messages. Right hand receptors will send a 'cold' message and left hand receptors will send a 'hot ' message. She will find it hard to tell how warm the water actually is.

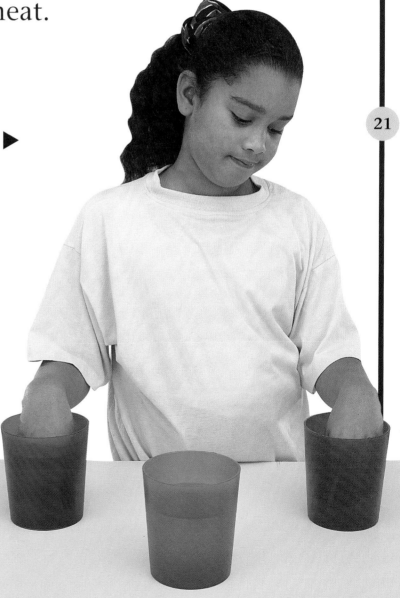

Pain

Pain is a warning signal to the body about something harmful, dangerous or unpleasant. It makes us do something to remove ourselves from the danger before any serious damage is done. It is important that we notice pain whenever it occurs so that we can react.

There are several types of pain. Some pain can be sharp and pricking. While other pain can be slow and burning or a deep ache.

There are different types of pain. A broken leg will ▶ probably feel like a deep ache. A thumb hit by a hammer will probably feel as if it is on fire!

We feel pain when our pain receptors respond to something. Pain receptors are free nerve endings. They occur in every part of the body except the intestines and the brain. Some parts of the body are much more sensitive to pain than others. Pricking the skin of your finger with a needle will cause pain, but the same needle used for an injection into a muscle will cause less pain.

▲
This athlete has stopped running because she has a painful injury.

23

Cleaning cuts and grazes ▶ properly may hurt more than the injury itself, but it will prevent **infection** and help healing.

Controlling Pain

There are many ways of trying to control pain. Some medicines, such as painkillers, can help to reduce pain. They do not take away the cause of the pain. They just alter the brain's reaction to the pain so that you are less aware of it.

▲

Before anaesthetics were invented, doctors tried other ways of putting patients to sleep

In hospital and at the dentist, **anaesthetic** is given to control pain. Dentists inject anaesthetic into the gum to make it numb before filling a tooth. A general anaesthetic puts a patient to sleep before an operation.

There are ways of reducing pain which do not rely on drugs. The Chinese system of acupuncture has been used for more than three thousand years. Special needles are inserted carefully into the body, in exactly the right places. The person is unable to feel any pain and doctors can carry out an operation. Nobody knows exactly why acupuncture works, but it may make the brain produce its own painkilling chemicals.

▲
Spraying a local anaesthetic onto an injury will stop the pain, but the athlete may make the injury worse by playing on.

◄ Many dentists use a local anaesthetic to make part of the mouth numb before they start any treatment.

When Things Go Wrong

Pain is not always felt in the same place as the injury or disease which causes it. For example, people suffering from some types of heart disease often feel pain in the left arm. This type of pain is called referred pain.

▲

Like this pirate, people with only one leg can sometimes still feel a pain in the other leg.

◄ This man suffering from heart disease may also feel pain in his left arm as well as in his chest.

Some people who have had a leg cut off still feel pain in it even though it is not there. This is called phantom pain. Doctors think it happens when nerve endings which connected the limb to the brain are stimulated. The brain thinks it is getting a message from the limb itself.

A few people cannot feel pain at all. This can cause many problems. Pain is really a signal warning us of something which may damage our bodies. Without this warning system, children who cannot feel pain have to be very careful. They could burn a hand and not even notice. They have to check their bodies regularly to make sure there is no damage.

If a child who cannot feel pain falls of ▶ their bike, they have to check their body carefully to find out if they are injured.

Animals and Plants

Other living things can feel things in the world around them.

Sharks have hundreds of tiny holes in their faces and along the sides of their bodies. These can detect very small electrical signals which other creatures give off, and small movements in the water. Sharks use the electrical signals and the water movements to pinpoint their prey.

▲
Cats use their whiskers to detect tiny movements in the air. They use them to pinpoint where something is.

◀ A shark can pick up tiny electrical signals and water movements.

Snakes have very sensitive heat detectors. Special holes on the sides of their heads can pick up the heat given off by warm-blooded animals. This helps the snake to locate its prey, even if it cannot see it or hear it.

Some plants are sensitive to touch. The Venus fly trap relies on touch to catch its food. When an insect lands on the end of a leaf, leaf hairs detect the movement. This triggers the leaf to snap shut, trapping the insect inside.

Leaves being touched.

Leaves after being touched.

▲ This sensitive plant called a mimosa curls up its leaves if you touch it.

Glossary

anaesthetic A substance that blocks feelings of pain.

capillaries Very small blood vessels.

cell One of the millions of tiny building blocks which make up your body.

dermis The inner layer of the skin.

ducts Tubes in the body which carry fluid.

epidermis The outer layer of the skin.

infection When germs get into the body and cause illness.

nerves Cells which carry messages to and from the brain.

pigment A substance present in the body that produces colour.

receptor A cell which reacts to a stimulus, sending a message to the brain.

sensitive Able to react to movement or change.

stimulus A change which affects a receptor.

vibration A tiny backwards and forwards movement.

Books to Read

For younger readers

Touch (Senses series) by Mandy Suhr and Mike Gordon (Wayland, 1993).

Touching and Feeling (Senses series) by Henry Pluckrose (Franklin Watts, 1997).

For older readers

Thinking and Feeling (Body Systems series) by Angela Royston (Heinemann, 1996).

Touch, Taste and Smell (Human Body series) by Steve Parker (Franklin Watts, 1989).

Index